FACTS AND
FICTION ABOUT
DRUGS™

MARIJUANA

CLARA MACCARALD

rosen publishing's
rosen
central

New York

Published in 2020 by The Rosen Publishing Group, Inc.
29 East 21st Street, New York, NY 10010

Library of Congress Cataloging-in-Publication Data

Names: MacCarald, Clara, 1979– author.
Title: Marijuana / Clara MacCarald.
Description: First Edition. | New York: Rosen Publishing, 2020 | Series: Facts and fiction about drugs | Includes bibliographical references and index. | Audience: Grades 5–8.
Identifiers: LCCN 2019013272 | ISBN 9781725347656 (library binding) | ISBN 9781725347632 (paperback)
Subjects: LCSH: Marijuana—Juvenile literature. | Marijuana—Physiological effect—Juvenile literature. | Marijuana—Therapeutic use—Juvenile literature. | Marijuana abuse—Juvenile literature.
Classification: LCC HV5822.M3 M193 2020 | DDC 362.29/5—dc23
LC record available at https://lccn.loc.gov/2019013272

Some of the images in this book illustrate individuals who are models. The depictions do not imply actual situations or events.

Manufactured in the United States of America

CONTENTS

INTRODUCTION

Governments across the world are relaxing laws around marijuana use. As of 2018, thirty-three US states, as well as the District of Columbia, legalized some form of marijuana use. Canada and Uruguay allowed recreational marijuana. Other countries, including Germany, Argentina, and New Zealand, permit limited medical or recreational use.

People have used marijuana for a long time. Its use as a medicine may have started thousands of years ago in Central Asia. Some groups may have used marijuana for religious purposes. Colonists in the Americas grew marijuana plants to produce fiber. By the 1800s, doctors and drugstores in Europe and America were giving patients medical marijuana.

In the next century, marijuana use became popular in Mexico for recreation and as a way to treat pain. Many Mexicans fled to the United States during the Mexican Revolution (1910–1920). They brought their smoking habit with them. Some Americans feared and hated these new arrivals. They complained that the Mexicans would take too many jobs. Because of racism against Mexican immigrants, Americans began to fear marijuana.

Newspapers spread stories about marijuana making users crazy. States began to ban it. In 1931, the Marijuana Tax Act banned recreational use of marijuana across America. In 1970, the federal government banned all uses. People still used and sold marijuana illegally. Much of the use of marijuana was recreational.

But marijuana appeared to help patients with medical conditions such as cancer or acquired immunodeficiency

Governments that legalize marijuana must figure out how patients will get the drug. They must create systems to allow people to produce marijuana and to sell it.

syndrome (AIDS). Because it was illegal, patients had to acquire the drug illegally if they wanted to use it. The public worried patients would miss out on a beneficial drug. In 1996, California legalized marijuana for medical uses. Other states followed.

Public opinion also held that marijuana was no more harmful than alcohol or tobacco. People used marijuana anyway, some pointed out, so why not use it legally? Governments and companies saw the chance to make money by selling and taxing the popular drug. US states began to allow recreational use of marijuana. But scientists are still learning about the real risks and potential benefits of the marijuana plant and its products.

CHAPTER ONE

All About Marijuana

Marijuana has many names. People call it weed, pot, dope, and cannabis, among other names. Marijuana is the most popular recreational drug. According to the National Survey on Drug Use and Health, 40.9 million Americans used marijuana in 2017. That is a lot of people. However, it's important to remember that most Americans (85 percent) did not use marijuana.

Whatever people call it, marijuana comes from a cannabis plant. Some scientists recognize two species of cannabis: *Cannabis sativa* and *Cannabis indica*. Other scientists argue that there's only one species, *Cannabis sativa*. Cannabis plants are flowering herbs. Some kinds of cannabis plants grow very tall and straight. Others are shorter and bushy. Cannabis plants contain chemicals that affect the human body. Cannabis originally grew wild in Asia, but people have now planted it around the world.

Over time, growers have bred cannabis plants to produce more of the qualities they want. Different strains have different amounts of marijuana chemicals.

The Chemistry of Marijuana

Marijuana contains hundreds of different chemicals. Some of the chemicals may be linked to cancer. Some may have health benefits. Marijuana chemicals occur in the leaves, stems, and flowers of cannabis plants. Different kinds of cannabis plants have different levels of chemicals. Many of the chemicals are released when people burn marijuana. Burning also creates tar and other substances not found in the plant itself.

Scientists, doctors, and marijuana users are mostly interested in two chemicals. These chemicals are called tetrahydrocannabinol

(THC) and cannabidiol (CBD). THC can cause users to become high. Although reactions to THC may vary, a person who is high typically feels relaxed and unusually happy.

Chemicals in marijuana such as THC and CBD affect the human mind and body. They are similar to chemicals the brain uses to control itself. These chemicals are called cannabinoids. Cannabinoids can increase or decrease the strength of the brain's

WHAT ABOUT HEMP?

Hemp is another name for the *Cannabis sativa* plant. However, when people talk about hemp, they don't mean the kinds of cannabis plants grown mostly to produce drugs. Instead, they usually mean a tall kind of cannabis grown mostly for the strong fibers in its stalks. Hemp plants can have CBD. But they have either no THC or very little THC. Smoking or eating hemp will not give anyone a high.

In December 2018, US laws changed so that hemp was no longer a controlled substance. The new law allowed farmers to grow hemp plants in the United States. Hemp grows very quickly. It is very strong. Farmers can make a lot of money with hemp. Industries can create many useful products.

Hemp products include rope, clothing, and paper. People can eat hemp seeds. Food companies add hemp seeds to products such as baked goods and granola. Processing can produce a kind of milk from hemp seeds. Processing hemp seeds can also produce hemp oil and hemp protein. Companies often use hemp plants to produce CBD oil. But while hemp is legal across America, CBD may be controlled by other laws.

signals. The parts of the brain affected by cannabinoids control processes in the body such as memory, thinking, and movement, as well as pleasure. Because the natural chemicals do so much, THC does more than get users high.

A person using marijuana might find an image more beautiful or important compared to when she isn't taking marijuana. Things she hears might sound funnier. Users may talk a lot. To someone who isn't using marijuana, the person might sound foolish.

A person who is high may not be able to keep track of time. She may have trouble thinking clearly or moving her body correctly. She may get very hungry. Users call this getting the munchies. Her mouth may become very dry and her eyes become red. She may become very tired.

Recreational users are looking for fun. Instead, they may have a bad experience. Users may feel anxious and scared. They can think things that aren't true. They may have trouble controlling their own thoughts. Marijuana users may feel paranoid. Paranoid means very fearful or worried someone will try to harm you. Users may even hallucinate. People using marijuana may feel so bad that they are in danger of harming themselves and may end up in the emergency room.

THC can make anyone feel bad instead of good. However, some things make a bad experience more likely. People who haven't used marijuana before are in more danger. So are people who mix marijuana with other drugs. Using a large amount of marijuana, or marijuana which is high in THC, is very risky.

The levels of THC in an individual plant depend on its type and how it's grown. The average levels of THC in marijuana have increased over time. According to the journal *Biological Psychiatry*, THC levels went up from about 4 percent in 1995 to about 12 percent in 2014.

Sellers like to package edibles in ways that make them look harmless and fun. The products look more like junk food than drugs

People are more likely to get into trouble when they eat marijuana rather than smoke it. Smoking usually has an effect right away. After eating marijuana, the effects may take one to three hours to hit. The effects also go away more slowly. People may eat too much and not know until it's too late.

CBD does not cause a high. People are interested in CBD because it may have medical uses without some of the dangers of THC. For example, people still report feeling relaxed just using CBD. Because the effect is milder, more governments allow the use of CBD than of marijuana itself.

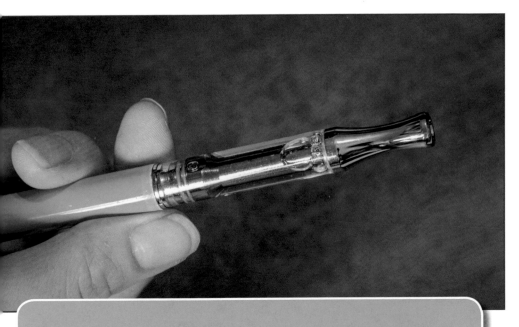

By lightly heating marijuana oil or other forms of marijuana, a vape pen puts chemicals such as THC into the air without making smoke.

Using Marijuana

To use marijuana, people put the chemicals from the plant into their body. There are several ways to do this. Some users breathe in marijuana smoke. The chemicals go into their bodies through their lungs. Users can also eat marijuana or marijuana products. When they do so, the chemicals come in through their stomach and intestines. Some marijuana products go on the skin.

People prepare marijuana in different ways. One way is to dry the leaves and flower buds. These parts of the plant are full of chemicals like THC. Dried marijuana burns. Burning it creates the smoke for users to breathe in. Users can make a cigarette with marijuana, which is called a joint. People can also use marijuana to make tea. They can eat it. Where marijuana is legal, some companies sell food or drink with marijuana or marijuana chemicals in it. These products are called edibles.

People also process the plant. They can harvest the resin to make a drug called hashish. Hashish burns like the dried plant. People can make marijuana oil from the plant. People can eat both hashish and marijuana oil. They can turn the oil into steam using a vaporizer. Using a vaporizer is called vaping. Vaping avoids some of the chemicals created when marijuana is smoked normally. But vaping creates stronger effects in users, which is risky.

To use marijuana as medicine, a patient might use marijuana the same way that a recreational user does. But it's hard to tell how much THC or CBD a piece of the dried plant contains. Treating a condition requires the use of measured doses. Labs

Growers often want larger plants with more THC. They may want a grow room to create the ideal conditions for marijuana plants by controlling things such as temperature and moisture.

can process marijuana to make useful medicines. They've created pills, mouth sprays, and creams.

Laws specify who can grow the plant and where. People might grow cannabis plants in fields, in gardens, or in special growing rooms. Growing rooms must provide their crop with strong lights and food. People who grow the plant illegally try to hide their crop from government officials.

Although a few marijuana users grow their own plants, most purchase the drug from someone else. Many users buy marijuana illegally. They may live where the government has banned marijuana. Users may also buy from a dealer without a permit.

Other users buy marijuana legally. If patients need medical marijuana, they may require a note from a doctor. Some states limit the use of medical marijuana to particular medical conditions.

In some places, the law allows special stores called dispensaries to sell marijuana. Buyers must be above the legal age. In the United States, that age is twenty-one, while nineteen-year-olds can buy marijuana in Canada. In the Canadian provinces of Alberta and Quebec, the legal age is eighteen. Buyers can buy only a limited amount. In parts of California, users can order marijuana online. Most companies deliver the drug directly to a buyer's home. When marijuana became legal in Canada in 2018, adults could buy small amounts through the mail.

In the United States, the federal government still considers marijuana a banned substance. Trade in marijuana can't cross state lines. The federal government doesn't control the quality or strength of marijuana for sale. State governments need to oversee the marijuana market. A lack of oversight can put users in danger. It can also keep patients from getting the most effective medicine.

Cure-All or Cure Nothing?

In the 1830s, an Irish doctor, Sir William Brooke O'Shaughnessy, was working in India. He tested the effects of marijuana. He found the drug helpful for certain diseases. He saw it calm fits (such as seizures and convulsions), reduce throwing up, and recover appetites. Doctors and druggists began giving out the drug. But in the 1800s, doctors used many drugs no longer used today. Some were useless. Some were harmful.

Medical marijuana sounds good. Supporters claim the plant helps a large number of conditions. Unfortunately, the research is incomplete for many of these claims.

Some patients and doctors aren't waiting for proof. In places where only medical marijuana is legal, people need a doctor's note. A doctor's note can also allow children to use marijuana. It can let a person have more marijuana than is legal for recreational use. But even with a doctor's say-so, there are risks.

DOS AND DON'TS

Do talk to your doctor about marijuana.
Doctors are probably familiar with the latest research on marijuana. They can tell you more about your particular health concerns in regards to marijuana.
Don't talk to a teenaged relative about marijuana.
Your siblings, cousins, or other relatives might know people who use marijuana. Their experience probably does not reflect all the things that marijuana can do.

Do read government websites.
Governments are supposed to look out for the public good. They consider the research. They try to educate people about the facts. They want to limit the harm done by legal and illegal substances.
Don't read the websites of companies that sell marijuana.
People who sell marijuana want to sell as much of it as possible. If they do talk about the risks, they will probably say they are unlikely. They may make claims that science does not support.

Do find books at the library.
A librarian can help you search for books from knowledgeable sources about marijuana.
Don't read magazines that make marijuana sound exciting.
The people who produce magazines about marijuana use may not worry about the risks around marijuana use.

Marijuana as Medicine

Marijuana is a drug. Some of its effects might help treat medical conditions. Supporters of medical marijuana claim it helps a variety of conditions, including Alzheimer's disease, an eye disease called glaucoma, and mental health problems. Doctors don't know if marijuana helps these conditions. They need to do more research. In some cases, marijuana may make the disease worse. Or the side effects could be worse than those caused by other drugs for the condition.

Scientists do know some very useful effects of marijuana. Marijuana relieves pain. It can calm upset stomachs and

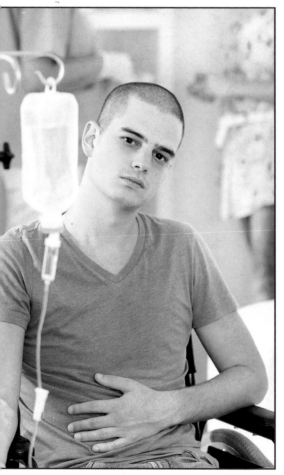

increase a user's appetite. It can also relax muscles. These effects are most promising for patients with AIDS, cancer, or multiple sclerosis (MS).

AIDS is a disease caused by the human immunodeficiency virus (HIV). HIV lives in a person's blood and other body fluids. The virus usually spreads through sexual activity or through shared needles. AIDS occurs when HIV damages a person's immune system. A weak immune system has trouble protecting a person's body. A patient with AIDS might get rare diseases or cancers. Doctors cannot get rid of HIV. But patients can take drugs to prevent HIV from causing AIDS, at least for a while.

Chemotherapy is a treatment that doctors use to try to kill cancer cells or stop those cells from growing. Scientists continue to research how marijuana may benefit cancer patients.

AIDs and the diseases that an AIDS patient may get can upset a person's stomach. It can make him throw up often. It can make him not want to eat. The drugs that treat HIV and cancer also can make someone very sick. Marijuana can help calm a patient's stomach. By making patients hungrier, marijuana can keep them from losing a dangerous amount of weight.

MS is a disease of the brain and nerves. It affects the way a person's brain communicates with her body. It affects the way her body works. MS can cause pain. It can make a person's muscles weak or stiff. Marijuana might relieve pain and make a person's muscles relax.

However, marijuana has side effects. For example, people with MS can have problems thinking clearly and remembering things. Marijuana use appears to make these problems worse. For an individual patient with AIDS and cancer, a different drug might work better.

One challenge with medical marijuana is getting the right dose. Marijuana plants vary in strength. Therefore, most marijuana products do as well. They have lots of chemicals as well as the one or two that help patients. Lab-made medicine can have the right chemical at the right dose.

Some countries have approved a mouth spray containing both THC and CBD. The spray treats pain and muscle problems. As of 2018, the Food and Drug Administration (FDA) had not approved the spray for use in the United States. However, it had approved a few others. Two FDA-approved pills contain human-made THC. They treat upset stomachs and lack of appetite in cancer and AIDS patients.

A liquid with CBD treats children with very bad epilepsy. Epilepsy is a disorder of the brain that causes seizures. For many patients, medicine can stop the seizures. But some patients

The quality of CBD oil on the market varies. For example, some CBD oil has more THC than the label claims.

continue to have seizures even when treated. More research may increase the epilepsy cases in which the liquid can be used. Other the other hand, research may also find that the liquid doesn't work very well.

Just as with marijuana, people claim CBD helps many conditions. Many American stores have begun selling CBD oil and food and drink with CBD added. Some people take CBD because they think it makes them healthier. Others are looking to treat conditions including pain, sleep problems, and anxiety. Other than with epilepsy, no research has shown that CBD works.

Support for medical marijuana continues to spread. Scientists are looking to the future. They're researching new possible medical uses for marijuana. Marijuana might also help treat people addicted to other, riskier drugs such as opiates. Early studies show marijuana might treat some cancers. It might even kill some cancer cells.

If this effect turns out to be real, doctors must find a way to understand and harness the ability of marijuana to fight cancer. Not all cancers are the same. Reaching a cancer with medicine can be very difficult. A cancer patient wouldn't be able to just smoke a joint. Still, drugs made from marijuana might someday benefit cancer patients.

A Note of Caution

Many people are rushing to use medical marijuana. Some doctors tell their patients to use the drug to treat all sorts of conditions. Some patients who use marijuana are convinced the drug is helping them. They don't care if there's no proof. These people may be experiencing the placebo effect.

The placebo effect can happen when people take a substance they think will help their health even though the substance has no real medical value. Somehow their condition improves anyway. Or sometimes the drug works, but it helps more than it should have. The person's belief in the substance made them get better. Scientists need research to tell the difference between the placebo effect and the action of a drug.

Even when a drug works the way doctors want it to, it can still cause side effects. Patients take a drug to treat a condition. Anything else the drug does to them is a side effect. Patients can overlook some side effects. Others can be very unpleasant.

Medical marijuana can cause several side effects. It can lead to depression. It can make the heart speed up. It can hurt

Although medical marijuana can be helpful in some circumstances, there can also be side effects, including mood issues such as anxiety and depression.

people's minds and lungs. Children and teens are most at risk. Patients who are very sick might also be more likely to be harmed by marijuana. They may already have a weak heart or lungs. If the patient is taking other medicine, marijuana might cause that medicine to work differently.

Just as with other medicine, people must follow their doctor's directions. Many kinds of medicine can have bad side effects. Doctors must decide if the possible benefits to the patient are worth the risks. More research will help doctors make those decisions about marijuana.

CHAPTER THREE

Where's the Harm?

The US government banned marijuana in 1970 because it thought the drug posed a great danger to the public. Despite the laws, lots of people used marijuana illegally. The public began to question how harmful marijuana really was. It didn't seem as deadly as heroin or cocaine. Scientists needed to study the issue in a controlled manner. But bans made the drug hard to study. Scientists needed special permits to work with marijuana. The lack of research made it hard to know what marijuana really did to recreational users.

As more governments legalize marijuana, science scrambles to keep up. Scientists are looking at how marijuana affects the brain and the body. They've found that marijuana is not as unsafe as governments once said it was. Legal marijuana has been linked to only a handful of deaths. In contrast, alcohol and tobacco kill large numbers of people every year. But scientists

US states that allow the sale of marijuana benefit from millions of dollars in marijuana taxes and fees. But states also need to be concerned about the health of their citizens.

have also learned marijuana poses real risks to users and to the public. In particular, the drug can harm children and teens.

Marijuana and the Brain

Marijuana affects the brain. When a person uses marijuana, the drug keeps them from thinking clearly or acting correctly. The effects can last a day or even two. For some, in particular people who start using at a young age, the effects can endure for much longer. Marijuana use might affect the way a young person's brain grows.

Using marijuana may make it harder for people to learn as they get older. They may have trouble remembering things. They may struggle with self-control. They might pay attention to the wrong things. Children whose mothers used marijuana while pregnant can have problems, too. They may be extra small at birth. They may struggle to learn and pay attention, as if they were using marijuana themselves.

Frequent use of marijuana or too much THC can make things worse. Scientists aren't sure if quitting marijuana can fix a person's brain. Still, it appears that some people function better after they've stopped using the drug.

Marijuana can affect a person's mental health. For some people, marijuana might cause anxiety or depression. People with anxiety worry a lot. They may not feel comfortable being in public. People with depression might feel sad, or they may feel numb. They might have no interest in things they used to love. The effect on mental health may be short-lived. Or it may last for a longer period of time. Scientists are still studying the issue.

For a small number of users, marijuana appears to cause mental disorders. Marijuana can trigger psychosis for a short

The increasing strength of marijuana and marijuana products on the market may be linked to more emergency room visits. Higher THC doses are more likely to cause mental problems.

period of time in apparently healthy people. Psychosis is a condition that affects a person's thoughts, feelings, and behavior. People experiencing psychosis seem to have lost touch with reality. They may hallucinate. They may talk without making any sense. They may act strange and be unable to do normal things.

Psychosis caused by marijuana might go on for a few hours or a week. For some, psychosis may last for months. This is more likely to happen to people taking a lot of THC or using marijuana often. It might even happen to someone who's never used marijuana before.

Marijuana use may also lead to schizophrenia. Schizophrenia is a disorder that causes a person to experience periodic

EDIBLE DANGER

Where marijuana is legal, edibles are linked to more problems than other forms. People who haven't used marijuana before or who have only smoked it may not understand how to eat marijuana. A food product such as a cookie may contain a large portion of marijuana. The user is meant to break off and consume a small piece. But people normally eat a whole cookie. They don't always pay close attention to directions. They can easily eat a risky amount of THC.

Edibles often look like normal candy or desserts. Children can unknowingly eat them. States have moved to make edibles safer. They've limited how much THC can be in edibles. They've also worked to change the packaging. For public safety, the packages must state clearly how to use the product. The packages can't be too colorful and appealing to children.

psychosis. Though rare, schizophrenia can be very harmful if not treated.

Scientists think it's possible that marijuana causes mental disorders only in people who are already at risk. Even if they hadn't used marijuana, they might have developed schizophrenia for a different reason. But scientists aren't sure. And people at risk for mental disorders probably don't know it. Marijuana could pose a danger to anyone's mental health.

Marijuana Problems

Marijuana can cause many problems. It can harm both users and the general public. Right after a person uses marijuana, it can make his heart speed up. A fast heart rate increases a person's risk for a heart attack. Some patients who want to use medical marijuana are very ill. Their hearts may be weaker than the average person's.

A person might not use marijuana on days she has school or work. But some of the effects can last up to two days. Using on the weekend might lead to problems during the week. Marijuana can cause a student to get worse grades. It can make a person perform poorly at a job.

Like tobacco, marijuana affects lung health. Marijuana smoke contains hundreds of chemicals, even more than marijuana itself. Users hold in the smoke longer than people using tobacco. The smoke puts tar into people's lungs.

Smoking tobacco greatly increases a person's risk of lung cancer. So far, marijuana has not been linked to lung cancer. However, using marijuana can create breathing problems. It makes users' lungs less healthy. It makes users more likely to get sick.

Marijuana can cause public health problems, too. It can increase the number of people visiting emergency rooms. In 2011, the Drug Abuse Warning Network estimated that almost 456,000 patients had used marijuana before visiting the emergency room.

RELIABLE RESOURCES

If a friend or family member is struggling with marijuana use or addiction, it can be hard to find sources of information and advice you can trust. Here are some places to go for help:

- **Substance Abuse and Mental Health Services Administration Helpline,** 1-800-662-HELP (4357), https://www.samhsa.gov/find-help/national-helpline. A twenty-four-hour service in English and Spanish that answers questions and connects Americans to places near where they live for help treating addictions.
- **"What to Do If You Have a Problem with Drugs,"** https://www.drugabuse.gov/related-topics/treatment/what-to-do-if-you-have-problem-drugs-teens-young-adults. A web page from the National Institute on Drug Abuse providing teens and young adults with answers about addiction.
- **"Get Help with Problematic Substance Use,"** https://www.canada.ca/en/health-canada/services/substance-use/get-help/get-help-problematic-substance-use.html. A website from the government of Canada with a list of helplines and services by province.
- **Kids Help Phone,** 1-800-668-6868: https://kidshelpphone.ca. A Canadian group that provides kids with options to call, text, or live chat about problems in their lives such as addiction.

Patients may have taken too much THC. They may have lung problems or mental health issues. Marijuana use might play a part in some car crashes. Often the driver was also using alcohol. The higher levels of THC found in marijuana sold today can make all of these problems worse. So can THC-rich products such as hashish.

A Question of Addiction

Some people who support marijuana argue that it's not addictive. They're wrong. People can become addicted to marijuana. Researchers led by Deborah Hasin studied responses to the National Epidemiological Survey on Alcohol and Related Conditions. In a 2011 study published in the journal *JAMA Psychiatry*, researchers found that 8.9 percent of marijuana users appeared to become addicted over time. People who start using the drug before adulthood are even more likely to become addicted.

People who are addicted to a substance have trouble stopping use of that substance. They may

Marijuana is an addictive drug and many users may have trouble quitting, especially if they started using before they were adults. It takes support and hard work to break the cycle of addiction.

need outside help to stop. Use of the substance harms their lives. It may keep them from acting properly at school, home, or at a job. For example, someone addicted to marijuana may use it on a school day. Yet getting high makes it hard to think clearly. She won't learn as well as students who don't use marijuana. People who are addicted may spend too much money buying the substance.

People who are not addicted to marijuana may still have a marijuana use disorder. People who quit but have a marijuana use disorder may long to use marijuana again. Their brains have learned to depend on the chemicals in marijuana to feel good.

Trying to quit marijuana makes people with a marijuana use disorder feel unhappy. They may even feel sick. While trying not to use marijuana, they may get annoyed easily. They may feel moody. They may have trouble sleeping. They may feel weak, be unable to relax, or sweat a lot. In 2012 and 2013, the National Epidemiologic Survey on Alcohol and Related Conditions-III found that almost three out of ten users qualified for a marijuana use disorder. People who start using marijuana as teens are more likely to develop a disorder.

CHAPTER FOUR

Street Smarts

In a growing number of places around the world, people can legally use marijuana. Although laws are relaxing, not everyone can or should use the drug. Marijuana can harm a person's health. Users can get into legal trouble. These problems are more likely when the user is underage. Because of the danger, laws restrict use to adults even where marijuana is fully legal.

Still, there are ways people can acquire marijuana illegally. Children or teens might have an adult buy the drug for them. They might buy from an illegal seller. Most people will have to make choices around marijuana use at some point in their lives. The choices they make can either protect them or put them in danger.

Risky Buys

One job of the government is to keep the public safe from the products they buy. Government officials test products on the market. They confirm the product is what the seller says it is.

MARIJUANA

They make sure the product is unlikely to pose a great risk to the buyer or to the public. When buyers complain about problems, the government is supposed to try to fix them.

In the United States, the federal government has trouble watching over the marijuana market. Marijuana is still illegal under federal laws. The federal government has stepped back to allow states to make marijuana legal. However, that means state governments have had to step up. They've had to decide how to oversee their marijuana markets.

The situation has led to an uncertain legal market. Legal marijuana products may not contain what the seller says they do. The strength of a product varies. Or its package may not fully explain how to use the product. A person looking to use recreational marijuana may take too much THC at once.

Marijuana products may not be pure. They can have chemicals left over from when the plant was grown. These chemicals could have come from fertilizers used to make the plant grow bigger, or pesticides used kill pests. The product might also have rot and bacteria.

While the legal market is risky, the illegal market is even riskier. The government does not control street marijuana. What sellers are offering may not be what they say it is. Harmful drugs may be added to marijuana. These drugs can give the user a far different experience from what he wanted. They could greatly harm a user's health.

Selling marijuana illegally is a crime. Someone willing to break the law may be committing other crimes. He may be an unsafe individual to know.

Some people call marijuana a gateway drug. They say that using marijuana leads a person to try other, more risky drugs.

FAKE MARIJUANA

Synthetic marijuana is a name for a risky group of drugs. "Synthetic" means human-made. Synthetic marijuana is a group of chemicals made in a lab. The chemicals are similar to those found in cannabis. The effect is often far worse. Synthetic marijuana can and does kill users.

Because it is not marijuana, some kinds of synthetic marijuana are legal. When it can, the government bans synthetic marijuana. However, people get around the laws by changing the exact chemicals. The law is always trying to keep up.

(continued on the next page)

Synthetic marijuana acts on the same parts of the brain as real marijuana. The synthetic marijuana also affects other parts of the brain, sometimes with unexpected results.

31

(continued from the previous page)

Like marijuana, synthetic marijuana has many names. Sellers might call it Spice, K2, or a hundred other terms. They might claim the product is natural. The packages are usually bright and exciting. Users may smoke the packaged drug. They might also make tea from it. Liquid synthetic marijuana can work in a vaporizer.

Some kinds of synthetic marijuana are stronger than THC. They're more likely to cause psychosis and make people hallucinate. They can make people want to hurt themselves and others. Synthetic marijuana can harm a person's organs. Whether it's legal or not, using synthetic marijuana is a risk that's not worth taking.

The research is mixed. Most marijuana users don't move on to using harder drugs. If they do, it may be because they already know someone who sells or uses illegal drugs.

Using a substance like marijuana changes the brain. It makes the brain more likely to enjoy other drugs. Marijuana users sometimes end up having problems with alcohol and tobacco, for example.

Legal Trouble

People looking to use legal marijuana need to know the rules. The laws are different in every country and state. No matter what US states say, as of 2018, the federal government does not allow the use of any marijuana. It doesn't matter if the use is recreational or medicinal.

Companies may test workers or people applying for a job for marijuana use. Those that test positive may be fired or lose their chance to be hired in the first place.

People should never trust others to know the law for them. The law may only permit medical use. It may require a doctor's note. If recreational marijuana is allowed, only adults can purchase and use it legally. Laws might limit the amount of the drug people can buy or have on them. Laws control where it can be used. Even adults may only be able to smoke marijuana on private property.

Marijuana can easily get people into trouble. The effects take a long time to wear off. A user may still feel them at work or school. She may perform poorly or hurt herself. If a job or a school finds out, the worker or student could get fired or expelled.

If people break the law, they might have to pay a fine. They may spend time in jail. A criminal record can make getting a scholarship or loan money for college more difficult. It could affect the kinds of jobs a person can do in the future.

THE WAR ON DRUGS

In 1971, President Richard Nixon declared a war on drugs. The government cracked down hard on recreational drug use. People of all races and levels of wealth use marijuana. However, the law went after black people more often than white people. Poor people had trouble getting good lawyers to fight in court.

Black communities in particular suffered. People ended up in jail for having small amounts of marijuana. They ended up with a criminal record. Even where marijuana is legal, the problem remains. Black people and other minorities are more likely to get into trouble.

Some people think the US government needs to help. The new rules around marijuana should help everyone, not just white people. People argue that jails should release people whose only crime had been using marijuana. People arrested for marijuana should no longer have a criminal record. Marijuana laws have been changing quickly. But change for people hurt by earlier laws has been slow to come, if at all.

Marijuana Choices

Some people have the chance to use marijuana legally. Children with health conditions may have the chance to use medical marijuana. Adults might live in places where they can use recreational marijuana. Other adults can visit places where recreational use is legal.

For those who do decide to use marijuana, there are ways to stay safer. Still, marijuana is a drug. Using it will always include some risk. People must decide if the benefits are worth the risk.

Patients should only use medical marijuana following the advice of a doctor. Any medicine can have side effects. When doctor suggests a medicine that has value to the patient, the doctor must consider the risks as well. These risks may be worse for people who are already sick.

The patient must follow the doctor's directions closely. Using too much marijuana causes problems. Even when a doctor suggests medical marijuana, a patient might decide he isn't willing to try it.

If adults have legal ways to use recreational marijuana, they can still keep themselves safe. They can wait until at least age twenty-five. Waiting will limit the harm marijuana can do to their

Legalization has made marijuana easier to get. Through marketing, companies make the drug seem cool and fun. Some fear that legalization leads to more marijuana use by young people.

brain. It also limits the likelihood of marijuana causing psychosis or schizophrenia.

When a person decides to try marijuana, she should buy only from legal sellers. Doing so gives her the best chance for a safe product. She should ask the seller how to use the product. She should follow all instructions. In general, she should use only a small amount. It's better not to use marijuana often.

Even if a person uses marijuana as safely as possible, he can still have problems. Smoking could damage his lungs. He might accidentally get too much THC and have a bad reaction. Or he could have a bad experience just by chance. He might become addicted. He might end up with a marijuana use disorder. The best way to avoid developing problems related to marijuana is to never try it.

ADDICTED Unable to stop using a substance without unpleasant effects.

ADDICTIVE Describing a substance that causes the user to believe he or she can't function without it.

ALZHEIMER'S DISEASE A disease that damages the brain and memory.

DEPRESSION Feelings of deep sadness or a loss of interest in life.

DISORDER A condition that is unhealthy or not normal.

DISPENSARIES Places where people prepare and give out medicine.

EDIBLES Food or drink that contains marijuana or marijuana chemicals.

EMERGENCY ROOM The part of the hospital where people go when they need to be treated right away.

GLAUCOMA An eye condition in which pressure increases in the eye, which may cause partial or total blindness.

HALLUCINATE To see things that aren't really there.

JOINT A cigarette made with parts of the marijuana plant.

LEGALIZED Made to be lawful in an area.

MEDICAL Having to do with medicine and diseases.

MENTAL HEALTH Well-being of a person's mind and emotions.

PLACEBO A useless medicine that only works because the patient believes it should.

PREGNANT Carrying a child inside one's body.

RECREATIONAL Done for pleasure, joy, or fun.

RESEARCH Study of an issue in order to find facts and learn new information.

RESIN A sticky substance that oozes out of plants.

SUBSTANCE A particular kind of material with certain features.

VAPING Breathing in vapor from a drug created by an electronic cigarette or other device.

VAPORIZING Changing a substance into a vapor.

Above the Influence
Center on Addiction
633 Third Avenue, 19th Floor
New York, NY 10011-6706
(212) 922-1560
Website: https://abovetheinfluence.com
Facebook: @AbovetheInfluence
Instagram: @abovetheinfluence
Twitter: @abvethinfluence
Above the Influence is a program of the Partnership for Drug-
Free Kids, an organization helping families deal with
substance use and addiction. Above the Influence has
resources and tips for teens, stories from real teens, and
chances to get involved helping other teens beat
substance abuse.

Be Smart. Be Well.
Health Care Service Corporation
300 E. Randolph Street
Chicago, IL 60601
(800) 654-7385
Website: http://habitstohave.org/index.htm
Be Smart. Be Well is a website created from support by the
Health Care Service Corporation. It provides online videos
and articles telling people's stories and providing expert
information on addiction and other health issues.

Canadian Centre on Substance Use and Addiction (CCDUS)
75 Albert Street, Suite 500
Ottawa, ON
K1P 5E7, Canada
(833) 253-4048
Website: http://www.ccdus.ca
Facebook: @CCSA.CCDUS
Twitter: @CCSAcanada
The CCDUS is a council that looks at addiction and substance
    use in Canada. It provides the public with research-based
    information online about substances such as marijuana.

Kids Help Phone
300-439 University Avenue
Toronto, ON
M5G 1Y8, Canada
(800) 668-6868
Website: https://kidshelpphone.ca
Facebook: @KidsHelpPhone
Instagram: @kidshelpphone
Twitter: @KidsHelpPhone
Kids Help Phone supports Canadian kids struggling with
    problems, whether the issue is drug use, bullying, or
    another concern. The website has options to find help
    through a phone call, texting, or live chat. The group can
    also connect kids to therapy or other professional help.

National Institute on Drug Abuse (NIDA)
6001 Executive Boulevard
Room 5213, MSC 9561
Bethesda, MD 20892

(301) 443-1124
Website: https://www.drugabuse.gov
Facebook: @NIDANIH
Twitter: @NIDAnews
NIDA is a US government institution that supports research on
    drug use and addiction and increases public awareness to
    improve the health of individual people and the general
    public. NIDA's website provides information on many
    commonly abused drugs, including marijuana.

Substance Abuse and Mental Health Services Administration
    (SAMHSA)
5600 Fishers Lane
Rockville, MD 20857
(877) 726-4727
Website: https://www.samhsa.gov
Facebook: @samhsa
Twitter: @samhsagov
SAMHSA is a US government agency that addresses substance
    abuse and mental health across America. SAMHSA runs a
    twenty-four-hour helpline (1-800-662-4357) that connects
    Americans to centers, organizations, and groups near them,
    which can help treat their problems with substance abuse
    and drug use.

Abramovitz, Melissa. *Understanding Addiction*. San Diego, CA: ReferencePoint Press, 2018.

Alexander, Richard. *What's Drug Abuse?* New York, NY: Kidhaven Publishing, 2019.

Allen, John. *Thinking Critically: Legalizing Marijuana*. San Diego, CA: ReferencePoint Press, 2015.

Brezina, Corona. *Alcohol and Drug Offenses: Your Legal Rights*. New York, NY: Rosen Publishing, 2015.

Currie-McGhee, L. K. *Teens and Marijuana*. San Diego, CA: ReferencePoint Press, 2016.

Hand, Carol, and Jodi Gilman. *Marijuana*. Minneapolis, MN: Essential Library, 2019.

Horning, Nicole. *Drug Abuse: Inside an American Epidemic*. New York, NY: Lucent Press, 2019.

Mooney, Carla. *The Dangers of Marijuana*. San Diego, CA: ReferencePoint Press, 2017.

Steffens, Bradley. *Is Marijuana Harmful?* San Diego, CA: ReferencePoint Press, 2017.

Ventura, Marne. *The Debate About Legalizing Marijuana*. Lake Elmo, MN: Focus Readers, 2018.

Bourque, Andre. "How Hemp and the Farm Bill May Change Life as You Know It." *Forbes*, December 17, 2018. https://www.forbes.com/sites/andrebourque/2018/12/17/how-hemp-and-the-farm-bill-may-change-life-as-you-know-it/#518e66c1694c.

Centers for Disease Control and Prevention. "A Closer Look: How Cannabis Impacts Health." February 26, 2018. https://www.cdc.gov/marijuana/nas/index.html.

Collins, John. "Why Are So Many Countries Now Saying Cannabis Is OK?" BBC News, December 11, 2018. https://www.bbc.com/news/world-46374191.

ElSohly, Mahmoud A., Zlatko Mehmedic, Susan Foster, Chandrani Gon, Suman Chandra, and James C. Church. "Changes in Cannabis Potency Over the Last Two Decades (1995–2014)—Analysis of Current Data in the United States." *Biological Psychiatry*. 79 (2016): 613–619. https://www.ncbi.nlm.nih.gov/pmc/articles/PMC4987131.

Hasin, Deborah S., T. D. Saha, B. T. Kerridge, R. B. Goldstein, S. P. Chou, H. Zhang, J. Jung, R. P. Pickering, W. J. Ruan, S. M. Smith, B. Huang, B. F. Grant. "Prevalence of Marijuana Use Disorders in the United States Between 2001–2002 and 2012–2013." *JAMA Psychiatry* 72 (2015): 1235–42. https://www.ncbi.nlm.nih.gov/pubmed/26502112.

Little, Becky. "Why the U.S. Made Marijuana Illegal." History.com, August 4, 2017. https://www.history.com/news/why-the-u-s-made-marijuana-illegal.

Lopez-Quintero, C., J. Pérez de los Cobos, D. S. Hasin, M. Okuda, S. Wang, B. F. Grant, and C. Blanco. "Probability and Predictors of Transition from First Use to Dependence on Nicotine, Alcohol, Cannabis, and Cocaine: Results of the National Epidemiologic Survey on Alcohol and Related Conditions (NESARC)." *Drug Alcohol Dependence* 115 (2011): 120-30. https://www.ncbi.nlm.nih.gov /pubmed/21145178.

National Academies of Sciences, Engineering, and Medicine. *The Health Effects of Cannabis and Cannabinoids: The Current State of Evidence and Recommendations for Research.* Washington, DC: The National Academies Press, 2017. https://www.nap.edu/read/24625/chapter/1.

National Institute on Drug Abuse. "Is Marijuana Safe and Effective as Medicine?" June 2018. https://www.drugabuse .gov/publications/research-reports/marijuana /marijuana-safe-effective-medicine.

National Institute on Drug Abuse. "What Is the Scope of Marijuana Use in the United States?" June 2018. https:// www.drugabuse.gov/publications/research-reports/marijuana /what-scope-marijuana-use-in-united-states.

Ross, Janell. "Legal Marijuana Made Big Promises on Racial Equity—And Fell Short." NBC News, December 31, 2018. https://www.nbcnews.com/news/nbcblk/legal-marijuana -made-big-promises-racial-equity-fell -short-n952376.

Substance Abuse and Mental Health Services Administration. *Drug Abuse Warning Network: 2011: Selected Tables of National Estimates of Drug-Related Emergency Department Visits.* Rockville, MD: Substance Abuse and Mental Health Services Administration, May 2013. https://www.samhsa

.gov/data/sites/default/files/DAWN2k11ED/DAWN2k11ED
/DAWN2k11ED.pdf.

Substance Abuse and Mental Health Services Administration. *Key Substance Use and Mental Health Indicators in the United States: Results from the 2017 National Survey on Drug Use and Health*. Rockville, MD: Center for Behavioral Health Statistics and Quality, Substance Abuse and Mental Health Services Administration, September 2018. https://www.samhsa.gov/data/report/2017-nsduh-annual-national-report.

US Food and Drug Administration. "FDA and Marijuana." June 25, 2018. https://www.fda.gov/NewsEvents/PublicHealthFocus/ucm421163.htm.

Van Vechten, Ellen. *On the Other Side of Chaos: Understanding the Addiction of a Loved One*. Las Vegas, NV: Central Recovery Press, 2018.

Wakefield, Jane. "Where Ordering Cannabis Is Easy as Booking a Taxi." BBC News, January 3, 2019. https://www.bbc.com/news/technology-46618262.

Walsh, Zach, Raul Gonzalez, Kim Crosby, Michelle S. Thiessen, Chris Carroll, and Marcel O. Bonn-Miller. "Medical Cannabis and Mental Health: A Guided Systematic Review." *Clinical Psychology Review* 51 (2017): 15–29. http://blogs.ubc.ca/walshlab/files/2015/06/Review-Article.pdf.

About the Author

Clara MacCarald is a freelance writer with a master's degree in ecology and natural resources. She writes nonfiction books for kids on topics ranging from history to science and technology. Her books include *Life with Epilepsy* and *Beating Bullying at Home and in Your Community*. She is a member of the Society for Children's Book Writers and Illustrators as well as the National Association of Science Writers.

Photo Credits

Cover MmeEmil/E+/Getty Images; p. 5 Africa Studio/Shutterstock .com; p. 7 photolona/Shutterstock.com; p. 10 Bob Berg/ Getty Images; p. 11 CAPJAH/Shutterstock.com; p. 12 Canna Obscura/Shutterstock.com; p. 16 vgajic/E+/Getty Images; p. 18 ElRoi/Shutterstock.com; p. 20 Jan H Andersen/Shutterstock .com; pp. 22, 35 Blaine Harrington III/Corbis Documentary/ Getty Images; p. 23 Photographee.eu/Shutterstock.com; p. 27 wavebreakmedia/Shutterstock.com; p. 31 Spencer Platt/ Getty Images; p. 33 KeyStock/Shutterstock.com; back cover and interior speech bubbles sumkinn/Shutterstock.com.

Design and layout: Nicole Russo-Duca; Editor: Jennifer Landau; Photo researcher: Sherri Jackson